THE

Also by Stephen Dunn

Between Angels

Local Time

Not Dancing

Work & Love

A Circus of Needs

Full of Lust and Good Usage

Looking for Holes in the Ceiling

Landscape
at
the
End
of
the
Century

W. W. Norton & Company

New York · London

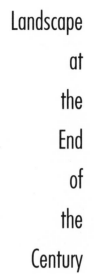

Landscape

at

the

End

of

the

Century

poems

Stephen

Dunn

Printed in the United States of America.

The text of this book is composed in Bodoni Book,
with the display set in Futura Lite Condensed.
Composed by PennSet, Inc.
Manufacturing by Courier Companies, Inc.
Book design by Antonina Krass.

First edition.

Library of Congress Cataloging-in-Publication Data
Dunn, Stephen, 1939–
Landscape at the end of the century : poems / Stephen Dunn.
p.   cm.
I. Title.
PS3554.U49L36   1991
811'.54—dc20   90–48701
ISBN 0–393–02972–7
W. W. Norton & Company, Inc.
500 Fifth Avenue, New York, N.Y. 10110
W. W. Norton & Company, Ltd.
10 Coptic Street, London WC1A 1PU
1 2 3 4 5 6 7 8 9 0

For Philip Booth

It is precisely what is *invisible* in the land, however, that makes what is merely empty space to one person a *place* to another.

—Barry Lopez

Clean out the heart.

—Richard Stern

Contents

Allegory of the Cave (1990)   15

Part One

Update   19
What They Wanted   21
The Woman on Edgehill Road   23
The Man in the Forest   25
Smiles   27
Midwest   30
Ordinary Days   32
Regardless   33
From the Manifesto of the Selfish   35
The Artist as Lefthander   36
Bringing It Down   37
White Collar   40
The Sudden Light and the Trees   42
On the Death of a Colleague   44
Turning Fifty   46
When the Revolution Came   48

Part Two

Nearing Midnight at the Century Club   51
Not the Occult   53
Elegy for My Innocence   56
Little Essay on Communication   58
Epithalamion   60
Good Talk   61
Stations   63
Working the Landscape   65
Drift   67

After the Resolution   70
A Secret Life   72
Pedestals   73
Ghosts   75
Landscape at the End of the Century   76

Part Three

Loves   81

Acknowledgments

These journals have published or will publish the following
  poems:
American Poetry Review: "What They Wanted"
The American Scholar: "On the Death of a Colleague"
Antaeus: "A Secret Life"
Boulevard: "The Man in the Forest"
The Georgia Review: "Bringing It Down," "Not the Occult"
The Laurel Review: "From the Manifesto of the Selfish"
New England Review: Middlebury Series: "Ordinary Days,"
  "Working the Landscape"
Organica: "Pedestals," "The Artist as Lefthander"
The Paris Review: "The Sudden Light and the Trees,"
  "Epithalamion"
Poetry: "Loves," "Landscape at the End of the Century," "Little
  Essay on Communication," "Stations"
Poetry Northwest: "Elegy for My Innocence"
Shenandoah: "Midwest," "After the Resolution"
Sycamore Review: "Drift"
Virginia Quarterly Review: "Update," "Regardless"

"On the Death of a Colleague" won the Mary Elinor Smith Prize
  from *The American Scholar.*
"Loves," "Landscape at the End of the Century," and "Little
  Essay on Communication" won the Oscar Blumenthal Prize
  from *Poetry.*

My thanks to Philip Booth, Lawrence Raab, and Carol Houck
  Smith for their close attention to many of these poems.
  Thanks, too, to the NEA for a fellowship, Stockton State
  College for its continuing support, and to Yaddo, where sev-
  eral of these poems were written.

Allegory of the Cave (1990)

He climbed toward the blinding light
and when his eyes adjusted
he looked down and could see

his fellow prisoners captivated
by shadows; everything he had believed
was false. And he was suddenly

in the 20th century, in the sunlight
and violence of history, encumbered
by knowledge. Only a hero

would dare return with the truth.
So from the cave's upper reaches,
removed from harm, he called out

the disturbing news.
What lovely echoes, the prisoners said,
what a fine musical place to live.

He spelled it out, then, in clear prose
on paper scraps, which he floated down.
But in the semi-dark they read his words

with the indulgence of those who seldom read:
It's about my father's death, one of them said.
No, said the others, it's a joke.

By this time he no longer was sure
of what he'd seen. Wasn't sunlight a shadow too?
Wasn't there always a source

behind a source? He just stood there,
confused, a man who had moved
to larger errors, without a prayer.

Part
One

Update

TO BARTLEBY

There is the sky and here
is the grass, he said to you,
but you couldn't be fooled.
Not much has changed.
Nearby is the slavish city
and once upon a time
there was a God.
You'd be among our homeless,
nameless and cold.
The elms are dead, and fires
have taken acres of pines.
You'd never be able to tell
that the ocean has changed.
Here is the wind
and there are the balloons
the children have let go.
I know where I am, you said;
office, prison,
all the same to you.
There's the path
up the mountain where often
bear tracks have been seen,
and here the tree on which lovers
carved their names.
First they grew apart,
then they died.
The bears were interested
in berries. Like you,
they kept to themselves.
Love would have changed

everything for you,
but Melville was wise;
you'd have been forgettable,
bringing the costly bacon home.
The imagination still opens the door
we hesitate before,
still turns on the light.
Here is the book
in which you live
and here's what you've spawned:
drop-outs, slackards,
and a kind of dignity, a quaint
contagious way to refuse.
In the face of decency
how did you see the absurd?
The system still shows
its sweetest face, still sends out
an honest man with a smile.
Here are the foul-mouthed
gorgeous gulls,
and these are the walls
in which we live,
in which your heirs
call themselves free.
It's the end of the century;
almost everyone dreams of money
or revenge.

What They Wanted

They wanted me to tell the truth,
so I said I'd lived among them
for years, a spy,
but all that I wanted was love.
They said they couldn't love a spy.
Couldn't I tell them other truths?
I said I was emotionally bankrupt,
would turn any of them in for a kiss.
I told them how a kiss feels
when it's especially undeserved;
I thought they'd understand.
They wanted me to say I was sorry,
so I told them I was sorry.
They didn't like it that I laughed.
They asked what I'd seen them do,
and what I do with what I know.
I told them: find out who you are
before you die.
Tell us, they insisted, what you saw.
I saw the hawk kill a smaller bird.
I said life is one long leave-taking.
They wanted me to speak
like a journalist. I'll try, I said.
I told them I could depict the end
of the world, and my hand wouldn't tremble.
I said nothing's serious except destruction.
They wanted to help me then.
They wanted me to share with them,
that was the word they used, share.
I said it's bad taste

to want to agree with many people.
I told them I've tried to give
as often as I've betrayed.
They wanted to know my superiors,
to whom did I report?
I told them I accounted to no one,
that each of us is his own punishment.
If I love you, one of them cried out,
what would you give up?
There were others before you,
I wanted to say, and you'd be the one
before someone else. Everything, I said.

The Woman on Edgehill Road

Ah, thinks the man, that woman walking
    Edgehill Road, weeping,
has a story to tell, what luck to find
    a woman like this.

All day he's wanted to tell *his* story,
    but he knows the woman
has the weight of tears on her side, the primacy
    of outward grief;

there'd be long listening before it would be
    his sweet time.
He's in his slow car, slow because he wants
    it slow—

last night's shouting and slammed door
    putting him on cruise.
The woman is gesturing now, speaking out loud.
    Once, no doubt,

the person she so hates was a god.
    It's not funny,
but isn't it always funny, thinks the man,
    to someone?

He would like to pull up close. "This is
    the sadness car,"
he might say, "and this the weeping seat
    and this the seat

where you keep things inside." And they
    would take turns
all the way into the next state
    where suddenly

they wouldn't need each other, so bored
    would they be with sadness
and themselves. But the man is burdened
    by the history of men,

by every man who's yelled or whispered
    from a car
on a road like this. He doesn't want
    to scare her

and, besides, he lacks charm when he's sad.
    When he's sad
everything sounds wrong. He accelerates
    into silence,

and will never tell his story as he might have,
    though why should anyone care?
Already it's lost as he turns into Weaver Lane
    toward home,

has become a little more orderly, understood.
    And the woman, too,
he's thinking that years from now
    her ugly trembling lip

will be steady, she'll remember this afternoon
    in the past tense,
all her pauses, everything she omits,
    will be correct.

The Man in the Forest

knows he'll die someday.
This is why he may do something
too bold. In fact he's lost
in the forest because he needed
to prove he wouldn't get lost.

The animals watch from the lips
of their holes.
They're as good at stillness
as the man is at talking,
and they are not confused

by the little hum of their hearts.
How they despise the man's dog.
What is this creature
that comes when it's called?
No telling what it'll do

just to please the man.
This man, though, intends no harm,
would gladly let a groundhog
be a groundhog for the rest of its life.
And the dog's only crime

is how it's allowed itself
to be influenced by love.
They're just lost, both of them.
The animals have seen this for years.
If it weren't for the dog

it would be entertainment, pure.
Even when one man finds his way,
another comes back,
walks in circles, draws such
foolish attention to himself.

Smiles

It was as if a pterodactyl had landed,
    cocky
and fabulous amid the earth-bound,

so it's not difficult to understand
    why I smiled
when I saw that Rolls Royce

moving slowly on the Black Horse Pike
    past the spot
where Crazy Eddie's once was.

Just one week earlier I'd seen a man,
    button-downed and wing-tipped,
reading *Sonnets to Orpheus* in paperback

at the mall's Orange Julius stand.
    My smile was inward,
I craved some small intimacy,

not with him, but with an equal lover
    of the discordant,
another purchaser adrift among the goods.

Sometimes I'd rather be ankle-deep
    in mud puddles,
swatting flies with the Holsteins,

I'd rather be related to that punky boy
    with purple hair
walking toward the antique shop

than talk with someone who doesn't know
    he lives
in *"Le Siècle de Kafka,"* as the French

dubbed it in 1984. The state of New Jersey,
    that same year,
refused to pay Ai for a poetry reading

because her name needed two more letters,
    which produced my crazy smile,
though I wanted to howl too, I wanted to meet

the man who made the rule, kiss him hard
    on his bureaucratic lips,
perhaps cook for him a scalding bowl

of alphabet soup. Instead we added two asterisks
    and the check came!
Four spaces on a form all filled in

and the state was pleased, which is why
    I'm lonely
for the messiness of the erotic, lonely

for that seminal darkness that lurks
    at birthday parties, is hidden
among hugs at weddings, out of which

smiles, even if wry or bitter, are born.
　　In the newspaper today
it says that the man who robbed a jewelry store

in Pleasantville, crippling the owner,
　　wasn't happy
with his life, was just trying to be happier.

And in Cardiff, just down the road, someone
　　will die at the traffic circle
because history says so, history says *soon*,

and that's the circle I must take
　　in my crushable Toyota
if I wish to stay on the Black Horse Pike,

and I do.

Midwest

After the paintings
of David Ahlsted

We have lived in this town,
have disappeared
on this prairie. The church

always was smaller
than the grain elevator,
though we pretended otherwise.
The houses were similar

because few of us wanted
to be different
or estranged. And the sky

would never forgive us,
no matter how many times
we guessed upwards
in the dark.

The sky was the prairie's
double, immense,
kaleidoscopic, cold.

The town was where
and how we huddled
against such forces,
and the old abandoned

pickup on the edge
of town was how we knew
we had gone too far,
or had returned.

People? Now we can see them,
invisible in their houses
or in their stores.

Except for one man
lounging on his porch,
they are part of the buildings,

they have determined
every stubborn shape, the size
of each room. The trailer home
with the broken window

is somebody's life.
One thing always is
more important than another,

this empty street, this vanishing
point. The good eye knows
no democracy. Shadows follow

sunlight as they should,
as none of us can prevent.
Everything is conspicuous
and is not.

Ordinary Days

The storm is over; too bad, I say.
    At least storms are clear
about their dangerous intent.

Ordinary days are what I fear,
    the sneaky speed
with which noon arrives, the sun

shining while a government darkens
    a decade, or a man
falls out of love. I fear the solace

of repetition, a withheld slap in the face.
    Someone is singing
in Portugal. Here the mockingbird

is a crow and a grackle, then a cat.
    So many things
happening at once. If I decide

to turn over my desk, go privately wild,
    trash the house,
no one across town will know.

I must insist how disturbing this is—
    the necessity
of going public, of being a fool.

Regardless

Once, my father took me to the Rockaways
    during a hurricane
to see how the ocean was behaving,

which made my mother furious, whose love
    was correct, protective.
We saw a wooden jetty crumble. We saw water

rise to the boardwalk, felt the wildness
    of its spray.
That night: silence at dinner, a storm

born of cooler, more familiar air.
    My father
always rode his delightful errors

into trouble. Mother waited for them, alertly,
    the way the oppressed
wait for their historical moment.

Weekdays, after six, I'd point my bicycle
    toward the Fleet Street Inn
to fetch him for dinner. All his friends

were there, high-spirited lonelies, Irish,
    full of laughter.
It was a shame that he was there, a shame

to urge him home. Who was I then but a boy
   who had learned to love
the wind, the wind that would go its own way,

regardless. I must have thought damage
   is just what happens.

From the Manifesto of the Selfish

Because altruists are the least sexy
    people on earth, unable
to say "I want" without embarrassment,

we need to take from them everything
    they give,
then ask for more,

this is how to excite them, and because
    it's exciting
to see them the least bit excited

once again we'll be doing something
    for ourselves,
who have no problem taking pleasure,

always desirous and so pleased to be
    pleased, we who above all
can be trusted to keep the balance.

The Artist as Lefthander

Each morning, thinking of you,
I rise from the counterworld of sleep
into those right-minded conventions
of day, so right I know
they must be wrong. Surely the world
belongs to others. Stick shifts.
Can openers. Definitions of decency.

I never recognize myself when America
gives back its images. The sitcoms,
billboards; sometimes I feel insane.
Only baseball with its beautiful word
southpaw has given me a proper name.
Southpaw. I'm about to attack, I'm
crouching in the woods with a name like that.

The other side, my advantaged ones,
is always angry, and is not dumb.
I've learned your language.
I've gotten in to your workplaces and your homes.

Bringing It Down

The man watched
   and though he was accustomed
     to what he saw

it struck him he was looking
   at a sky
     that could hold a jet

and no longer a god.
   And against decency,
     for reasons

he didn't want to know,
   he began to bring
     that jet down,

the plane getting larger
   as it descended
     out of control,

a fire in the fuselage,
   then the few lives
     he'd help save.

The man simply wanted to feel
   at ease, that's all.
     That's how he thought:

first some wildness, then
a healing ease.
He wanted one person

he'd brought down
to be whole,
smiling up at him,

her seatbelt still on.
He brought on
the dark clouds.

From where he stood
he brought them
from the west

and the noise began.
What harm
in a little more damage?

He brought the wind, the hail.
There weren't enough
rewards in this world,

he felt, for the things
he imagined,
but didn't do.

The man went inside.
He had some
unanswered letters

on his desk. One he'd never
    answer because it was
        too detailed and thoughtful,

full of a love he couldn't match.
    He'd save no lives,
        he thought.

Even if he rummaged
    through the wreckage, everyone
        would be too far gone.

He put the letter in a box
    of letters, the box
        he expected to astound him

when he was old. The lost, the dead
    would speak to him then.
        He'd make sure of that.

White Collar

He has to put it somewhere, the violence
    from without. Each day
it comes from newspapers and the streets,

so ordinary now it lives with white lies
    and spoiled milk,
yet it amazes him how easily it mixes

with his own, that there's a place for it,
    located no place
in particular, just part of him

like fat—rapes, tortures, massacres,
    all taken in
and covered by nerve endings half dead.

Oh, once he had feelings equal to what
    he should feel,
in the old neighborhood, years ago . . .

He's a citizen, but now always
    of somewhere else,
the marshland pushing him to the city, the city

to the mountains, the enormous country itself
    inclining him inward
to his room with its shelves of private anthems.

He believes that someone intimate with need
    and scarcity,
crack-driven, knife-happy, nothing to do

until the pawnshop opens, is moving randomly
    in his direction.
It's inevitable, this touch of the personal.

In his violence place, a stirring, as if his body
    and its repressed
outlaw history might be readying itself

for action. But that person never arrives,
    chooses a darker house
with the gate open, no sign of a dog.

The Sudden Light and the Trees

Syracuse, 1969

My neighbor was a biker, a pusher, a dog
    and wife beater.
In bad dreams I killed him

and once, in the consequential light of day,
    I called the Humane Society
about Blue, his dog. They took her away

and I readied myself, a baseball bat
    inside my door.
That night I heard his wife scream

and I couldn't help it, that pathetic
    relief; her again, not me.
It would be years before I'd understand

why victims cling and forgive. I plugged in
    the Sleep-Sound and it crashed
like the ocean all the way to sleep.

One afternoon I found him
    on the stoop,
a pistol in his hand, waiting,

he said, for me. A sparrow had gotten in
    to our common basement.
Could he have permission

to shoot it? The bullets, he explained,
    might go through the floor.
I said I'd catch it, wait, give me

a few minutes and, clear-eyed, brilliantly
    afraid, I trapped it
with a pillow. I remember how it felt

when I got it in my hand, and how it burst
    that hand open
when I took it outside, a strength

that must have come out of hopelessness
    and the sudden light
and the trees. And I remember

the way he slapped the gun against
    his open palm,
kept slapping it, and wouldn't speak.

On the Death of a Colleague

She taught theater, so we gathered
in the theater.
We praised her voice, her knowledge,
how good she was
with *Godot* and just four months later
with *Gigi*.
She was fifty. The problem in the liver.
Each of us recalled
an incident in which she'd been kind
or witty.
I told about being unable to speak
from my diaphragm
and how she made me lie down, placed her hand
where the failure was
and showed me how to breathe.
But afterwards
I only could do it when I lay down
and that became a joke
between us, and I told it as my offering
to the audience.
I was on stage and I heard myself
wishing to be impressive.
Someone else spoke of her cats
and no one spoke
of her face or the last few parties.
The fact was
I had avoided her for months.

It was a student's turn to speak, a sophomore,
one of her actors.

She was a drunk, he said, often came to class
reeking.
Sometimes he couldn't look at her, the blotches,
the awful puffiness.
And yet she was a great teacher,
he loved her,
but thought someone should say
what everyone knew
because she didn't die by accident.

Everyone was crying. Everyone was crying and it
was almost over now.
The remaining speaker, an historian, said he'd cut
his speech short.
And the Chairman stood up as if by habit,
said something about loss
and thanked us for coming. None of us moved
except some students
to the student who'd spoken, and then others
moved to him, across dividers,
down aisles, to his side of the stage.

Turning Fifty

I saw the baby possum stray too far
and the alert red fox claim it
on a dead run while the mother watched,
dumb, and, oddly, still cute.
I saw this from my window
overlooking the lawn surrounded
by trees. It was one more thing
I couldn't do anything about,
though, truly, I didn't feel very much.
Had my wife been with me,
I might have said, "the poor possum,"
or just as easily,
"the amazing fox." In fact
I had no opinion about what I'd seen,
I just felt something dull
like a small door being shut,
a door to someone else's house.

That night, switching stations, I stopped
because a nurse had a beautiful smile
while she spoke about triage and death.
She was trying to tell us
what a day was like in Vietnam.
She talked about holding
a soldier's one remaining hand,
and doctors and nurses hugging
outside the operating room.
And then a story of a nineteen-year-old,
almost dead, whispering "Come closer,
I just want to smell your hair."

When my wife came home late, tired,
I tried to tell her
about the possum and the fox,
and then about the young man
who wanted one last chaste sense
of a woman. But she was interested
in the mother possum,
what did it do, and if I did anything.
Then she wanted a drink, some music.
What could be more normal?
Yet I kept talking about it
as if I had something to say—
the dying boy
wanting the nurse to come closer,
and the nurse's smile as she spoke,
its pretty hint of pain,
the other expressions it concealed.

When the Revolution Came

When the revolution came we were lounging at home.
They were suddenly dancing in Prague
and we were setting the table, forks on the left,
knives on the right. All our categories were old.
We should have been making love when the Wall
came down. We should have been turning a phrase.
When the revolution came it was the widening of a crack,
the lifting of gray. The tyrants just stepped down.
Some apologized. History turned in its enormous grave.
When the revolution came we were wearing
the work boots of the miner, the downy vest
of the longshoreman, thinking of style.
When the revolution came we were counting
our deprivations as only the full-bellied can.
Walesa raised his hands in triumph. Our throats
tightened. East Berliners strolled into the land
of commerce; our throats tightened again.
Were we thinking of ourselves when the revolution
came? And did we feel a little smug?
It was a cold December when the century changed,
colder for some. It was not yet Christmas,
not yet Romania, that harsh gift, blood-soaked,
its past opened up. Every year we promised
to want a little less, and always failed.
When the revolution came we watched the insistence
of crowds, almost free enough to become us.

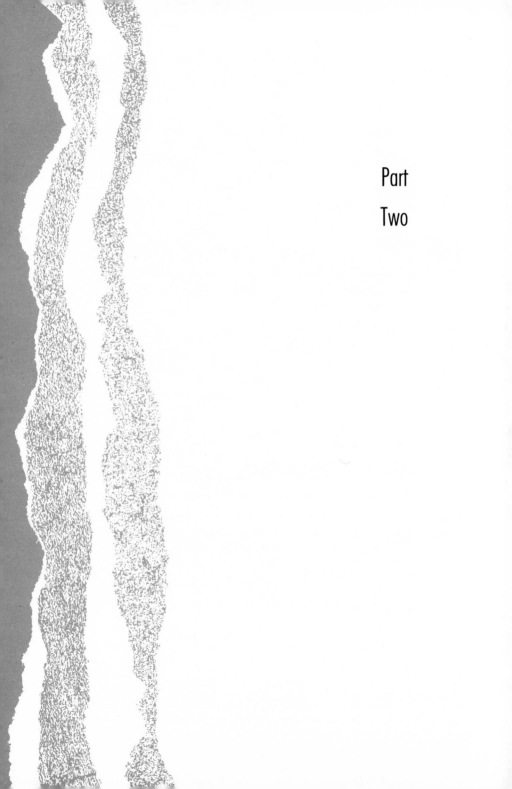

Part

Two

Nearing Midnight at the Century Club

It was nearing midnight at the Century Club,
all of us were dancing but not touching,
and it was clear that for some, the dazzling ones,
the sex this was leading to would be
anticlimactic, insufficiently various, just
a way to wind down. You and I, however,
had been thinking of something radically slow,
dreamy perhaps, fox-trot old. We moved
toward our seats, the strobe lights
coloring us stark white, jittery blue.
Hard as it was to speak over the music,
we actually felt like speaking,
that's what misfits we were, I wanted
to tell you about the virtues of pretense,
and you, as you later confessed,
wanted to speak about Gorbachev,
the little map on his balding head,
and how that map was the secret
but obvious key to how people live
exiled in their own country.
Then somebody from off the street
grabbed the mike to tell us all
we were dying, but he didn't do it in song
and was booed until he left,
even we booed him for such failure
of taste and timing, and were happy
when the lead singer took over again,
felt some odd comfort in his incoherence,
his anarchic repetitions. "Let's go,"
you said, "before we won't want to go,"

and we walked out of the Century Club
into the sensate, starless evening,
my hand bridging your waist and buttocks,
your hand in my pocket,
and we knew that things would feel new
for a while, which was all that we wanted.

Not the Occult

Because I was slow with girls
and didn't understand
they might like to be touched,
my girlfriend took my hand
and placed it on her breast.
We were sixteen. I just
left it there
as if I were memorizing,
which in fact I was.
It was all research and dream,
some fabulous connection
between my hand and her breathing,
then I was breathing like that too.

I've always been drawn
to such ordinary mysteries, women
and men, the broken bridge
between us. I like thinking
about night falling in a house
where anything can happen, and has,
strangers coming in
from their public outposts,
the drift of history
behind any wish to explain.
How to say what can't be said
across a table, or bed?

It's not the occult
and those obvious stakes
in the heart

that make me wonder.
And I confess
I have trouble speaking to people
fond of outer space.
I don't like riddles.
I'm tired of ambiguity's
old academic hush. Still . . .

things happen,
and simply to record them
is often to deceive,
is even sometimes to mimic fog,
the way it's perfectly
yet inadequately clear about itself.

I'm thinking of that woman
returning from the restroom,
unable to recognize her husband.
She wasn't old, he hadn't disappeared,
though she perhaps had lost him.
Where is my husband? she asked the waiter,
who pointed toward the table.

And I'm thinking of the time
we lay ourselves down
among the dwarf pines,
looked up at the sky.
Nothing was new up there,
and down here the words for love
stuck in their history of abuse.
Angel, I wanted to say, meaning darling,
it seems heroic how we survive each other,
heroic that we try.

I'm thinking of the power of loveliness
to sadden.

Oh once there was such awe,
such a pure desire to praise.
There's not one of us
who inspires as much.
But I love the local and crude
somehow made beautiful, all the traces
of how it got that way erased.
And I love the corporeal body itself,
designed to fail,
and the mind, the helpless mind,
so often impelled to think about it.

Elegy for My Innocence

You always stumbled in,
came out smelling
not quite like a rose.

Your most repeated gesture:
the blush.
You didn't know how to hide.

I do not miss you, but experience
is the guest
who only knows how to stay.

You, at least, were built to go,
which is why you can be loved.
I remember everything you craved.

Interesting, how you were diminished
by whatever you got. Sex,
knowledge, you kept going up in flames.

Each year you became
a little more dangerous,
eyes wide, the same poor reflexes

for pain. I last saw you
in Texas, 1963. No need by then
for a goodbye. Yet I've heard

that at the end of a long passage,
a lifetime, something like you exists,
terrifying and desirable,

and that no one who hasn't sinned
ever arrives. Innocence,
we could be such friends

if that were so. I'd start out now
if I didn't know
the lies told in your name.

Little Essay on Communication

Safe to say that most men who want
    to *communicate*,
who would use that word, are shameless

and their souls long ago have drifted
    out of their bodies
to faraway, unpolluted air.

Such men no doubt have learned women
    are starved
for communication, that it's the new way

to get new women, and admission of weakness
    works best of all.
Even some smart women are fooled,

though the smartest know that to communicate
    is a form of withholding,
a commercial for intimacy while the heart

hides in its little pocket of words.
    And women use the word too,
everyone who doesn't have the gift

of communication uses it.
    It's like the abused
asking for love, never having known

what it feels like, not trusting it
　if it lacks pain.
But let's say a good man and a good woman,

with no motives other than desire
　for greater closeness,
who've heard communication is the answer,

sign up for a course at the Y,
　seek counseling,
set aside two hours in the week

for significant talk. What hope for them?
　Should we tell them
very little, or none at all?

As little or none as there is for us,
　who've cut
right to the heart, and still conceal,

who've loved many times well into the night
　in good silence
and have awakened, strangely distant,

thinking thoughts no one should ever know?

Epithalamion

For a second marriage

If you, X, take this woman, Y,
and if you, Y, take this man, X,
you two who have taken each other
many times before, then this
may be something to trust,

two separate folks not becoming halves,
as younger people do, but becoming
neither more nor less than yourselves,
separate *and* together, and if
this means a different kind of love,

as it must, if it means different
conveniences and inconveniences, as it must,
then let this *good luck*
from a friend act like grease
for what may yet be difficult, undefined,

and when the ordinary days of marriage
stretch out like prairie,
here's to the wisdom which understands
that if the heart's right
and the mind at ease with it

the prairie is a livable place, a place
for withstanding all kinds of weather,
and here's to the little hills,
the ones that take you by surprise,
and the ones you'll need to invent.

Good Talk

Something to drink helps, of course,
    and humor must live
even on that dark corner where once

your life was threatened. Something in the voice,
    in the telling,
must signal *I am safe now and trying*

to please you, the wink not in the eye
    but in the phrase, the tone.
And seriousness must be taken for granted

like the hard work that makes the dinner party
    feel effortless.
Let at least one listener be contrary,

another famous for his honest, delayed assent,
    a traveler
of the same boulevards and alleys,

demanding you either be charming or exact.
    It will be
his turn soon, or hers, maybe something about

the pointless ferocities of intellectual life
    told from the inside,
which reminds everyone of a story.

Let all the laughter be perfectly pitched.
　　And the newcomer,
whose fine silence you've convinced yourself

is intelligence, has just taken a breath.
　　You'll not be forgiven
for speaking to her privately.

Stations

"That's not what love feels like,"
the radio psychologist said
to the battered woman

who insisted her husband loved her.
And I, voyeur in stalled traffic,
unable to stop

listening, stop anything,
heard the woman begin to weep,
a clean knife

of truth in her now.
It had begun to rain
as it often does in movies

when the hero discovers
his private heart
can't accommodate one more thing,

but my heart was enormous
in its greed, and the heavy rain
had nothing to do with me.

Though when she said,
"He's good to me, mostly,"
even I'd had enough,

so easy to imagine the rest,
how he'd confuse her with tenderness,
stick an apology in her face.

I switched stations
and in the suddenly synchronous morning
Tina Turner was singing

how Proud Mary "popped a lot of pain
down in New Orleans,"
bad husband Ike's deep

authenticating voice
in the background.
I was on the Parkway now, my wipers

metronomic, annoyingly good.
"What's Love Got to Do with It,"
was the next song

and Turner was so confident,
so raspily bold,
she left the question mark off.

Working the Landscape

They've taken me to a small lake surrounded
    by large, dead trees.
Gypsy moths, they say. Voracity.

They're taking a little too much pleasure
    in this. The day
is overcast, the water gray as a gun.

The night before they reintroduced me
    to their marriage.
It was like being invited to dinner

by people who are fasting: May we offer you
    a little spectacle
with your dessert? I'm their friend,

and they were loveless and unlovable.
    I listened, and went to bed.
Now these trees, dendritic, a bunch

of nerve endings reaching skyward.
    Isn't it beautiful,
they say, and it *is* beautiful

as often pollution is as it swirls
    from smokestacks.
But I don't wish to agree. I'd prefer the sound

of idiot birds, or that a crane swoop down
    prehistorically, begin to fish.
I tell them I've begun to love sunsets

and people walking off into them. I love
    old melodies, and melody itself.
They're smart enough to get my drift.

They stop working the landscape, stop, awhile,
    beating themselves up.
A tern dives and makes a tiny efficient splash.

And then the rain comes, the rain comes
    angel-driven to distract.
There's only that sound now—

desolate, heartening, whatever each of us wants.

Drift

One of those nights so quiet
    you can hear silence
but not your heart. Your heart's

the nightwatchman asleep on the job,
    underpaid,
unable to get another job.

Someone is dialing your number,
    you can sense it,
and once again your senses are wrong.

In the book you're reading there's a man,
    an amputee
who's found religion, given up

one of two delusions about women.
    You'd like to care.
What music should accompany silence?

Haven't you always orchestrated
    your life?
Deep down, you know it's mostly bad

to make a pact with God. There are
    better deals,
a few weeks in Bimini, a month perhaps

alive amid the fires, which for a while
   don't burn. Pay later,
not an altogether unhappy thought.

If there's an eternity, you tell yourself
   you'll suffer anyway,
as you do with anything that won't stop.

To have four walls around you
   should be comforting.
But you have more than four walls.

You can hear the refrigerator in the act
   of being cold,
and you approve. You're thinking about love

and you can't hear your heart
   and the universe, if you
dare wonder about it, doesn't care.

In that book you're reading someone knocks
   on the man's door.
She's misunderstood his message;

it's all so sad. *Touch me*, you hear
   yourself saying,
words tend to confuse. You're speaking

to the person who hasn't dialed. Once
   you actually knew someone
for whom time was money.

Is that what it means for a soul
   to be impoverished?
The night is young, the youthful say.

In a different time you would kiss
   their wide-open eyes.
You would praise their noise.

After the Resolution

He wanted to live as if he had one year
    to live,
which meant letting death sharpen

his day with its wonderful call
    to alertness, its link
to eros and all the sweet trouble

between fingertip and nipple,
    pen and page.
So he'd remind himself he was born

to startle, to disturb and please,
    that his work, for example,
awaited him like an open mouth,

and that the best way to rise in this world
    was to hunker down,
go deeper in. But after a while

his body wanted only to sleep,
    that's what
he discovered way down in himself,

the call of sleep, nearly as strong
    as death,
immediate, endurable. Beyond will,

he gave into it, mornings, afternoons,
  and always he met
another self there who had stopped

at all the stopping places, well-groomed
  stasis
in a terrifying suit and tie.

When he woke he'd try to forget
  what he had dreamed,
and, now, trying to forget once again,

sunlight filled the room like some divine
  lie, the dog sidled up
next to him, he felt so . . .

He wanted to steal other men's wives.
  He wanted to pick locks
and enter and destroy and rearrange.

And he wanted to sleep. Ahead of him:
  all the antipathies
of civility and desire, various forms

of silence, exchange. How
  to always keep
a promise? Doesn't the soul tire

of decency? Lunch was still to come
  and courage would be needed,
if he could muster some, to get dressed.

It had started to snow. A few cruel birds
  took over at the feeder,
bluer and handsomer than all the rest.

A Secret Life

Why you need to have one
is not much more mysterious than
why you don't say what you think
at the birth of an ugly baby.
Or, you've just made love
and feel you'd rather have been
in a dark booth where your partner
was nodding, whispering yes, yes,
you're brilliant. The secret life
begins early, is kept alive
by all that's unpopular
in you, all that you know
a Baptist, say, or some other
accountant would object to.
It becomes what you'd most protect
if the government said you can protect
one thing, all else is ours.
When you write late at night
it's like a small fire
in a clearing, it's what
radiates and what can hurt
if you get too close to it.
It's why your silence is a kind of truth.
Even when you speak to your best friend,
the one who'll never betray you,
you always leave out one thing;
a secret life is that important.

Pedestals

Surely the way she appears—
  as the only passenger
in an airplane piloted by a corpse—

is unnerving. But the dreamer is a man
  of course, on the outside
looking in, carrying a letter bag

marked Air Mail. He will die soon
  in the stratosphere
if he can't get in. He knocks

on her window, and the woman says
  to herself, *It's hailing,*
a storm has started, I'll close my eyes.

The dreamer knows an automatic pilot
  has taken over.
It's the end of feeling, there's nothing

to do but stare. He keeps asking,
  in the name of beauty,
Why is it so cold? To whom does she respond?

Every letter in his bag is addressed to her,
  each one *Urgent,*
covered with exotic stamps.

All he can think of as he loses his grip
  and falls
into the vague blue of wakefulness

is that she can never come down, the stupidity
   of it, this window
between them every night, and men like him

always putting planes like this in the air.

Ghosts

We who've hung around, living
    for an afterlife
       or a later-life,
who've mistaken the normal breeze

in the pines for applause,
we who've denounced the crows

for reminding us of our shadows,
    who've become old
       having become
so good at betraying our dreams

that we've called it service
to family, obeisance to Commandment,

it is we who'll be the ghosts
    compelled to return
       to the scenes
of our hesitations, our denials,

whose soundless laments—as if screamed
    from a different world—
       our disquieted children
will sense as something in the air.

Landscape at the End of the Century

The sky in the trees, the trees mixed up
with what's left of heaven, nearby a patch
of daffodils rooted down
where dirt and stones comprise a kind
of night, unmetaphysical, cool as a skeptic's
final sentence. What this scene needs
is a nude absentmindedly sunning herself
on a large rock, thinks the man fed up
with nature, or perhaps a lost tiger,
the maximum amount of wildness a landscape
can bear, but the man knows and fears
his history of tampering with everything,
and besides to anyone who might see him
he's just a figure in a clearing
in a forest in a universe
that is as random as desire itself,
his desire in particular, so much going on
with and without him, moles humping up
the ground near the daffodils, a mockingbird
publishing its cacophonous anthology,
and those little Calvinists, the ants,
making it all the more difficult
for a person in America
to close his office, skip to the beach.
But what this scene needs are wisteria
and persimmons, thinks the woman
sunning herself absentmindedly on the rock,
a few magnificent words that one
might want to eat if one were a lover
of words, the hell with first principles,

the noon sun on my body, tempered
by a breeze that cannot be doubted.
And as she thinks, she who exists
only in the man's mind, a deer grazes
beyond their knowing, a deer tick riding
its back, and in the gifted air
mosquitoes, dragonflies, and tattered
mute angels no one has called upon in years.

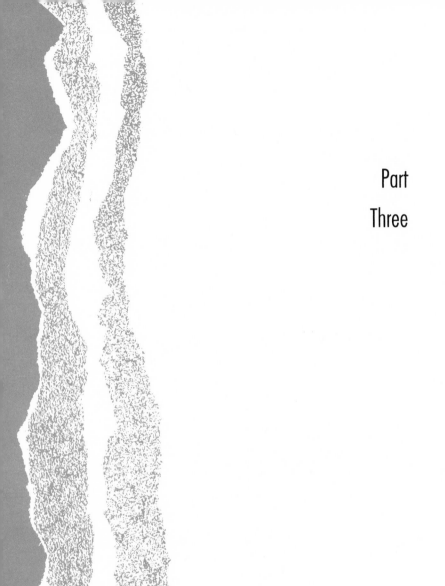

Part
Three

Loves

I love the past, which doesn't exist
until I summon it, or make it up,
and I love how you believe
and certify me by your belief,
whoever you are, a fiction too,
held together by what? Personality?
Voice? I love abstractions, I love
to give them a nouny place to live,
a firm seat in the balcony
of ideas, while music plays.
I love them more than hard evidence
and shapely stones, more than money,
which can buy time, but not enough.
I love love, for example,
its diminishments and renewals,
I love being the stupidest happy kid
on the block.
        And what's more interesting
than gossip about love? When I tell
a friend that my life is falling apart,
what a subject for him
to dine out on! What secrets for him
never to tell a soul, except those
souls to whom he tells everything.
I love how a good story insists
on being told.
    When I betrayed, I loved chaos,
loved my crazed version of sane.
When I was betrayed, I loved fidelity,
home. I love more carefully now.

But never to have betrayed, admit it,
is a kind of lethargy or rectitude,
a failure, pure.
        I love the way my cat Peaches
brought the live rat to the door
looking for praise. I love his dignity
when he seeks company, or turns away.
Of all fruits, plums.
Of vegetables, mushrooms sauteed
in garlic and wine.
I love that a list like this
always must extend itself,
and must exclude, slash.
Loving: such a ruthless thing.
        I love shifting from second
to third, that little smooth jerk
into speed, though it's not exactly speed
I want, but being in the middle of speed
as in the somewhere of good sex,
those untimed next things
occurring on time. I love the moment
at the races when they're all in the gate,
such power
not yet loose, and I love the race itself,
how the good jockey tempers and saves,
then dares. I love something to yell for,
something to bet my sweet life on
again and again.
        I love the ocean in winter,
that desolation from which I can return,
solitude that's sought and cradled,
the imaginings one leans toward
at a jetty's end. Often, out there,
I've remembered what I love

about my marriage, turns and gatherings,
odd sacrifices, the sticking it out.
In retrospect, and only in retrospect,
I love a cataclysm that heals.
I love knowing that a marriage
must shed its first skin
in order to survive, must shed again.
Wreckage, thy name is progress.
It hurts just to think of you.
        I love the power
not to use power, the weaker wolf
offering his jugular
and the stronger wolf refusing.
I love how breasts curve and reach
different crests, the long nipple, the
minor crown, the hard unbuttoned button,
each a gift. The faith we put
in a lover's mouth! I love when
a distinction vanishes
between infantile and adult.
     How alert I am to circumstance
when I'm leaving for a while,
or being left. I love the psychology
of kisses at such times, the guilt kiss
and the complaint kiss, the kiss
with a question in it.
And who doesn't love to be the one
who returns, all puckered and alive?
       I love the game-winning shot
that isn't an accident, the shot prepared for
all one's life, practice and talent
metamorphosed into a kind of ease.
I love the trouble
skill can get you out of, and the enlivening

pressures of boundaries and time.
No moment as lovely as the surpassing moment!
Oh poetry, oh the importance of ground
when leaving the ground.
      I love the carpenter bees
in spring, mating in air, and I don't mind
the holes they make in my house
or the innocent buzzing of my head.
Murderer, you're just a sting away.
Murderer, it's you who loves that weasel
in Nova Scotia, the graceful
treacherous one. Amazing
how he got through the chicken wire,
slinky as a mouse.
I love thinking of him returning
to the sanctuary of weasels, calm,
matter-of-fact. And something else in me
loved the blue jay
who all summer dive-bombed my cat,
the only justice it could deliver
for many blue deaths.
      "I want to be consistent
with the truth as it reveals itself
to me," Gandhi said, and I felt
the hard permission right words give us
to disobey, to become ourselves.
I loved thinking that integrity
might be fluid, and still do,
though the indulgent, rudderless
and without shame, love to think so too,
and the truth is
the indulgent are my careless brothers
half the time.
      I love the way sorrow and lust

can be companions. I love the logic
of oxymorons, and how paradox helps us
not to feel insane. Aren't facts
essentially loose, dull? I love
that an accident that doesn't occur
is replaced by one that does.
It's the personal that makes things count,
steadies a fact into importance. Otherwise,
there it is among the moon rising,
a piece of paper being torn, starfish
at the bottom of the sea.
        Interesting how long it's taken me
to discover fulfillment
can be more trouble than it's worth.
Interesting, that as desire recedes
the world becomes pale yet clear.
I love knowing that even in rapture
part of the mind watches, amused.
        I love that there's a secret
behind every secret I've ever told.
I love twelve-year-old scotch.
Before confessions of any sort,
a martini with a twist.
I love the wines
in my friend John's cellar,
the act of going down
and bringing them up,
and his vocabulary of taste
and aftertaste—tannin,
bouquet, tart—
I love how true experts speak
precisely, embody all the words.
And a beer for the big guy
at the end of the bar. He's my friend

too, on my father's side.
I love him for some old hurt
he's here to relieve.
            Who isn't selfish enough
to love zoos? Flamingos, baboons,
iguanas, newts.
Surely evolution has a sense of humor.
Surely the world would be something to love
if it weren't for us, insatiate,
our history of harm.
How hard even to love oneself,
all those things I've done
or dreamed of. Those vengeances.
            I love Don who is poor,
but I don't love the poor. I love *Jules
and Jim* more than I love *Casablanca*,
but only when I'm asked.
Isn't fairness for the timid?
I love the exacting prejudices
of the passionately thoughtful,
mercy earning its name,
transcending pity, which keeps
everyone small.
            I love my daughters out of
habit and conviction, my wife
for the long, undulating wave
of our friendship,
a few other women, a few men.
I love the number of people you can love
at the same time, one deep erotic love
radiating even to strangers, crippling
cynics, making a temporary sense
of the senseless, choreful day.
    When students fall in love with me

I want to tell them
I'm the dream that won't last;
there are more pleasures in the text.
So much eros in a normal room!
I love to use it
to make complexity joyous,
to heighten simple points.
    In spite of their lack of humor
I love Thoreau and Jesus, Marx,
Malcolm X. I love their obstinate courage,
Hunger Artists all, going forward
because the food they ate
tasted wrong, and the world was sad.
But I love the other heroes more,
Shakespeare and Picasso, Dickinson,
Beckett, Frost, wise dark players
among entropy and the ruins.
    I love the just-mowed grass
in spring, that good revision,
the clean odor of accomplishment.
I love the whale I saw
in the Caribbean, enormously itself.
And the fox who works the woods
behind my house, the envy of all of us:
deception without guilt.
I love the summer I decided to drive west
in a bad car.
I love the ferocity of certain dreams,
boulevards I've walked at midnight,
vulgarities made holy
in the mutual church of our bed.
    Those who've gotten away from me:
read this, and call.
Those whom I've hurt:

I wanted everything, or not enough;
it was all my fault.
    I love how the fireweed
came up on Mount St. Helens
through the crust of ash—
I think of this when my knees hurt,
when I feel like making an excuse.
I love that tyrants give birth
to the knives that slit their throats.
And I love the vigilant
who try to keep the tyrants dead,
knowing they rise with different names.
    (I'm saying all this to you,
my fiction, my one thing
that can be whole. I love what I might say,
the not yet felt or known.
In you there's room
for spires and orange rinds,
the mumbled, the suppressed.
In you I could get lost.)
    I love the manners of jazz musicians,
the playing off of and the taking turns,
and the formality of chamber players,
I love that too, the tuxes and deep bows,
and the little aristocracy of the first
violinist and the conductor, the audience
complicitous, desiring such a world.
I love how pop songs seem profound
when we're in love,
though they wound us too sweetly,
never seriously enough.
I love the good home
clichés can find in an authentic voice.
        I love the secret life

of hornets, famous for their sting,
all day at home making paper,
building a place they must leave.
I love the night-blooming cereus
for its name alone,
and the amaryllis
that must be kept in the dark,
and once a year
blooms brilliantly large.
Just be natural, the innocent say.
Such latitude!
Permission to be wild, bizarre.

I love intimacy, and accept
that concealment springs from it,
some partition of the heart
closing as it opens up.
After I asked my wife to marry me,
I hid behind a bush the next day
so she wouldn't see me,
and was thankful to Poe
and his Imp of the Perverse,
thankful, as it were, for a colleague.
Later, I loved telling her this,
laughter the sweetest agreement,
more conclusive than any yes.

To give succor to the dying
and to kiss the diseased. To put a coin
in a leper's hand, and to hold that hand.
I love such love, and am its failure.
I love the selfless, but they're no fun,
like faraway planets,
shining, always shining.
I prefer a vanity that can be appealed to.
I love room enough not to be good.

But what a pleasure it is
to feel righteous.
So rarely do I raise my voice,
what a pleasure to rant.
How seriously I'm taken then! Words
as bullets, emblems of the heart . . .
language every woman understands.
      I love to replace God
with all things tactile, responsive,
and I love artifice,
which is a way of being godly
if the product is good.
And science, its cures and its bomb;
I love with a fearful love
how far the mind has gone.
         Of all insects,
the thousand-legger.
Of flowers, the rose,
I cannot help it, the rose.
I love house more than country,
country more than space.
I love the thing chosen
and I love the illusion of choice.
        After the eyes offer up
their shynesses and deceits,
I look to mouths for the truth.
I love to see how temperament collects
in a smile, and often, before it happens,
it's possible to see cruelty,
a thin wire bent almost to a grin.
I love how lipstick can suggest
a grammar, and how, in sleep,
the mouth gives up its posture
like something defeated.

Isn't a morning kiss, then,
a kind of restoration, a love test
for the one who wakes first?
I love what we must forgive.
  So good to find them, the people
who've discovered fraudulence
in their lives, who've cast off, say,
a twenty-year lie.
I love how they listen to poems
as if words were necessary
daggers or balm, their faces proof
that the soul feeds on wild riffs,
every sort of truth-scrap, the blues.
I love that the normal condition
of the soul is to be starved.
      Of all seasons,
early autumn, the trees holding on
to what's theirs, and how nice
nobody's flunked yet, the classroom alive
with the beautiful ignorance of beginnings.
I love that the shy ones
sometimes grow wings,
and that the peacocks disappoint
when they begin to speak.
      I love to disappear on committees,
sneak out when the fastidious
begin to clean. I love to drift off
to where you are, love, when the solemn ones
need to make something clear.
Once in Chicago at the Hilton I slipped
an "I quit" note under my boss' door,
took a night flight home.
Whatever I love about my life
started there.

When it comes to mixed feelings,
I love when the undertow begins,
as it must, to work against the flow.
Last week, accused of duplicity,
I knew I was guilty
of loving too few; there are truths
that can't be said out loud.
It's the singleminded who get
the most done, who rush right in.
I love a little hesitancy
before the plunge.
Liars, the whole lot of us.
      I love looking
for that slow car around 10 A.M.,
the mail-woman, Dorothy, who knows
I live for acceptances
and declarations of love.
Sometimes I'm out there waiting—
Thursday—the best day,
as any connoisseur knows.
I love how she leans out of her Nova
with the steering wheel on the right.
I love that she apologizes for junk,
that she knows the feel and look
of the personal, and how mock-sad she gets
when she has little to give.
Sundays I think of envelopes
being licked and stamped, mail in
transit, dream-mail,
change-one's-life mail. Sunday,
worst day of the week. And those
church bells ringing *stasis, stasis.*
      In the spacey boredom
of late afternoon, I love

that the casinos are open and near,
and sometimes after midnight, too,
for indulgence or danger's sake,
I love to walk through those electric doors
into the quick comfort
of slot sounds and sleaze.
I love to take my place among the prodigal
escapees screaming for sevens,
and one big time when everything went
my way, I loved placing all that cash
on my wife's sleeping body,
loved, come morning, to see her waken
like that, covered with luck.
                    I love the hour
before dinner, cheese on the cutting board,
white wine for her, something hard
for me. I love the rituals that bring us
together when sullenness persists,
how the dishes must be done,
the children helped toward bed.
I love how familiar bodies drift
back to each other
wordlessly, when the lights go out.
Oh we will die soon enough.
Not enough can be said
for a redemptive caress.
    How good it's been to slide back
the heart's hood awhile, how fortunate
there's a heart and a covering for it,
and that whatever is still warm
has a chance.
I'm withholding things of course,
secrets I'll replay, alone,
when my bones get soft.

Even you have no place for them,
my spacious one, you who have existed
to resist me as I've made you up.
Do I sense you getting tired now?
Listen, my truest love, I've tried
to clear a late-century place for us
in among the shards. Lie down,
tell me what else you need.
Here is where loveliness can live
with failure, and nothing's complete.
I love how we go on.